PRAISE FOR *Cypher Garden* by Mary Kay Rummel

At times when I'm stuck or fall out of love with the world, I re-read her (Rummel's) poetry. Sometimes her words stir the space of what's missing in my life. Other times, when I'm on the edge of finding that love again, her poems give me courage. Though I may not be quite there yet, her work can re-affirm that loving embrace of who I am.

—Jean Colonomus, Poet, Playwright, Essayist

CYPHER GARDEN

ANSWERING STONE
THE VOICES
OF WATER

HOLY OILS
EMBLEMS OF EARTH
AMONG STARS

Poems by
Mary Kay Rummel

BLUE LIGHT PRESS ◆ 1ST WORLD PUBLISHING

1st WORLD
PUBLISHING

SAN FRANCISCO ◆ FAIRFIELD ◆ DELHI

ACKNOWLEDGMENTS

Thank you to those editors who selected these poems, sometimes in different versions, for publication.

Askew, The Gift, Symphony in Blue and Yellow

Banfill-Locke Museum Chapbook, Letter to Vincent

BoomerLitMag, First Fruit, Season of the Swan

Ekphrastic Review, Song of Clay, Lascaux

Gyroscope Review, On Water, In Air, Beyond the Hedge

Lummox, Out of My Hands

Miramar, The Roaring, The Open Window, Haiku Ladder

Nimrod, Cypher Garden, Vegetable Soul

St. Paul Almanac, Roaring Up West Seventh, Of Trains and My Father

Packinghouse Review, By Way of Words, Wild Tongues

The Poeming Pigeon, Reverse Migration

At the Table: Poems, Dining Room Table: Ways of Seeing New and Nearby Reading Series

Amore: A Collection of Love Poems, Johnny Tucker (ed), Baptist

Amethyst and Agate: Poems of Lake Superior, Holy Cow! Press, Welder

Carrying the Branch: Poets in Search of Peace, Glass Lyre Press, Remembering Paris: White Nights

Creativity & Constraint, Wising Up Press, Haiku Ladder

Laureate's Choice, Maria Faust sonnet competition: Baptist

THANK YOU TO THOSE WHO HELPED MAKE THIS BOOK POSSIBLE:

Colleen McCallion, for the cover painting, *Resting Mother*;

Melanie Gendron, Designer for Blue Light Press books for the design and the beautiful black and white drawings;

My husband, Conrad, for his continuing strong support;

Sandy Rummel for her advice;

Maia who has read so many of these poems in various stages and whose insight into poetry is continually amazing;

Diane Frank, Editor in Chief of Blue Light Press who inspired and helped shape the poems. This book would not exist without her generosity and insight;

Members of the Blue Light Press online workshop group who read much of this work in early stages;

Thomas R. Smith, Lois Jones, Marsha de la O, KB Ballentine and Jean Colonomus for their blurbs for this book;

Members of the Onionskin writing group, Patricia Barone, Sharon Chmielarz, Carol Masters, Nancy Raeburn, Margaret Hasse, and Ethna McKiernan; also Kate Dayton and Roseann Lloyd;

The Ventura County Arts Council who appointed me the first Poet Laureate of Ventura County;

Phil Taggart, Marsha de la O, Friday Lubina, Fernando Salinas, Gaby LeMay, Nancy Jean Pement, and Becky Sanvictores;

Jackson Wheeler, in gratitude and memory;

The Ventura Thursday night poets and all the hosts who have invited me to read;

Elizabeth Quintero and all the people who come to readings and buy books.

Thanks always to my family — Tim, Miranda, Sylvie and Bridget, Ann, Andrew, Mari and Libby for their inspiration.

FOR BRIDGET CLAIRE

CONTENTS

ANSWERING STONE

THE VOICES

OF WATER

HOLY OILS

EMBLEMS OF EARTH

AMONG STARS

Answering Stone

Cypher Garden

St. Olav Cathedral, Trondheim

1

On the flagstone floor
a carved garden dedicated to the deadly sins.
Each sin signed by an animal
an inverse sky of bestial constellations.

Gluttonous fat pig, low to the ground,
razor clawed crab secreting anger,
sweet sloth loving total laziness.
Empty squares demand sinners lay down
each transgression, stamped upon.

2

Whoever made animals emblems of sin?
I tried but couldn't think of deeds
in my long life I would quash.
My commitment to appetite,
crème brulee, provençal wine,
a bouillabaise of taste and smell?
Finding sun my home of slow dreams?
Butterflies connect the patchwork
of my anger, soaring into the spheres,
pigments from the warm body of the earth.

3

The animals in my cypher garden
fly in Chagall's vision, at the center of all things,
red whirling in a womb of yellow,
dancing bull and cow, flying fish, firebird,
Adam and Eve laughing
as they are expelled by a tender angel
flying out of and into hope.

4

I was twenty-six when I left the convent,
not knowing how my clumsy body could rise,
then fall like a feeding pelican, guttural moaning
in blue backed, red rimmed ecstasy.
Was it a sin, I asked a priest?
I don't know, he said.

5

Too many years before I flew into my body.
I would stamp on that sorrow—
its cypher was a blank slate.
What came after floods the margins.
Emblems in lapis, in carnelian.
Colors in the language of cardinals.

Think of the statue of the black bear
nosing a berry bush at the entrance
to Madrid's Puerto del Sol.
I was that beary appetite
and the sweet fruited bush.
I was so hungry.

The Roaring

St. Paul Zoo, 1955

A tide of noise, animal screams
beat against my head,
rocked the popcorn wagon,
swallowed whole the fountain
spraying its water wildly.

Seals barked in their pool.
Monkeys combed and combed
stopping to pick out nits.
I breathed in familiar musk,
wet fur, urine, bleach.
I thought I was safe,
when the roar rose up again
full-throated, gnawing, scarlet.

When my brothers called,
Let's find the lion!
running to the far corner
that held his cage,
I refused, wanting nothing
of muscled litheness pacing
a tiny, hosed-down space,
raw meat scattered on the floor.

These days I drag a chain
of *nos* and *not yets*.
When my vision wavers
with distance, I hear a drastic music
as through a wind tunnel.
If I could bellow yes like that
lion wave of blood-red fury,
my heart knows I would.

Deer For Her Birthday

Standing on the porch
in the frigid air
she saw a shivering doe
limned in white
watching her
across the snow
beneath the hunter's moon.

This morning she heard it
on the radio—
deer in the city.
It's turning even colder.
She is turning
growing back her fur.

She remembers sunlight on waves
how she threw her coins
from the pier into the ocean
emptied out her purse.

Last night a quiet fox
laid a careful track
behind her house
on the hard moon pond
scooped by wind.

Deer in the doorway
a well of joy inside her.
She prays the night will only steal
what she can afford to lose.

Thundering Up West Seventh

Along the Mississippi, sagging houses,
narrow streets discharge teens
born during the war or just after.
Lilacs droop over sidewalks,
scent the edges of drive-in parking lots.

Saddle shoes crush fallen blossoms,
scarves circle our junior high faces—
bright lips and cheeks, nylon knots
on our chins, badges of sophistication.
We eye the boys in fish tail Chevies,
watch older girls balancing trays—
root beer, burgers, deep fried onions.

In a cloud of greasy vapor, motorcycles roar
up West Seventh from the Harley Davidson shop.
My disbelieving stare trails Cookie and Rose,
their short bleached hair and leather jackets,
arms wrapped around the waists
of favorite bikers while crows in bare oaks
intone, *You can't   You can't.*

One night big Dave offers me a ride.
On his huge black Harley, my long braid flying
in that joyous wind, I cling to him
senses open like mouths shouting *Yes!*

Yes! to the long tongue of the road
lolling out before me.
Yes! to West Seventh transformed to ridge
across hills, shining Agean below.
Yes! To a white trail up mountains
where moose dance through drifts of snow.

Yes! to the clouds blooming lavender.
Yes! to grand bazaars and cobbled streets.
No! to staying home, my mother's anger,
my brothers' fights.
My pulse like a stadium of fists
punching *Yes! Yes! Yes!*

Later, I walk with Kathy and Sharon
past dark, crowded bars
ankle deep in tenderness and lilacs,
the roar of Harleys in my blood.

Haiku Ladder

Haiku saves lives. (Sonia Sanchez)

It gets inside you
deep like the blues, and deeper,
a river rising.

I was a young nun.
My mind hiked through syllables
beast hungry for words.

I could buy one book.
My twentieth year Basho
fell like a ripe plum

into my desperate hands.
His poems mirrored my mind.
Simply alive with them

I grew Haiku eyes.
The short lines slipped from my hand
flew into the world.

May evening shower
petals from the wild rose bush
moon light on the ground.

My thrown rock, became
Basho's frog plopping lidless
into convent pond.

Water rings exploded
silver dancers leapt shoreward.
Inside and outside

green growing wood weeds
covered the eyes of the priests
"Recall you are dust…"

The winter white pine
gives ice a place to hang on.
So haiku saved me.

In These Feral Times

Deep into my life, I'll be a she-wolf,
rough pelt smelling of polar winds
as my yellow eyes glean the night.

I'll bare my teeth, jagged as a bread-knife.
I'll be an outcast, a stranger
in this hinterland I prowl.

If you hear panting when I run
beside you, you think it's only
your own laboring, lonesome breath.

I'm your shadow loping in the glare
of headlights down a long road.

I shy away from the speeding truck.
The men inside with shotguns hunting
something free and silver under the moon.

Across the tundra of backyards and bushes,
I'll track the lost scents of my ancestors,
claim their territory as my own.

I'll walk in my own paw prints,
my howls echoing in the lake bowl,
even if I fool no one.

Girl Before a Mirror

(Picasso – 1932)

In the mirror she sees inside herself.
It's being back in the womb—
those walls of red, purple pink belly.
Inside her a yellow seed
grows into a plum.

In her hand she holds two stones
one a rose sweet light,
sunset sea close to shore;
the other a deep lapis,
soul tightening ocean.
Breaking the blue stone in half,
she gives it to her sister in the mirror.

Think of me, she says,
when you put them side by side.
Think of me in the dark mirror of your eyes.

Face cracked, lips parted.
The inside of a red satin slipper.
I tell you we are all someone else.

First Fruit

Not the serpent
but the vine—

the way it curls around her
tendriled toes and fingers

strong around her calf, around her thighs
as it writhes across her stomach

the newly formed still tender ribcage.
Clusters of dusky luminescence

press close
to her breasts, her arched neck.

She opens her mouth
to the sweetly tantalizing

to bitterness, sour greenness,
forbidden vermillion,

fermented honey,
over ripe peony, shriveled age.

She tastes them all
and blesses them.

Remembering Paris: White Nights

When you remember me, conjure Paris,
the clack of red high heels
in the night courtyard below our spiraled stairs.

You won't remember what I wore,
red dress with blue sash.
I remember your French,
voice warm, like a balm,
your eyes that deep end blue
color playing zither on my heart.
I saw the sea in them,
grace light of sun on waves
the shores we would follow.

Night after light filled night, we walked
along the Seine with our children.
Timothy talked beside us,
Andrew ran ahead scouting for *glâce*.
Later, in the small apartment bed
I lay with my head on your chest.
Even now, some savor of me wanders
narrow Paris lanes clinging to those aureate nights.

Symphony in Blue and Yellow

The whole thing will be a symphony in blue and yellow.
(Van Gogh, 1988)

1

Right now the world seems bleak —
wars grind on, children without refuge,
friends sick with cancer.
Rainclouds for a parched landscape
stray too far north again.

And here I am by the sea with you,
silver haired man who likes to be with me, still .
     How many times have I forgotten to give thanks?

In the West silver boats with black sails
that look like the backs of leaping whales.
One with crimson sails stretches its wings.
Round quarter notes of dolphins
dot the lavender page of sea.
Declouded sky boils at low flame.
     How foolish we have been
     to waste a single breath arguing!

Palm branches rustle, clouds of finches rise.
I know sorrow is somewhere out there,
but still the wing beats of my lungs inhale,
my blood sea blue in the tide of my heart.
Thirsty palms breathe in what I exhale,
wave their green fronds in gratitude.

2

Sometimes a dove on the boardwalk
comes as close to us as trust.
Its long vowels not mournful,
but one of those sounds that tap
into memory's underground river,
hill town in France, sun a rough-tongued cat,
citrine licking arms and faces.
Walking into a Van Gogh wheat field,
his symphony in blue and yellow.

3

"I am in it with all my heart," Vincent wrote to Theo.
I am in it too, this life with its longing,
its wide sorrows and slender songs.

If I am beautiful, it's because of your hands
moving over me, your lips saying my name.

We breathe with the sea, seraphic blue of the islands,
sun and moon in the same sky.

Catechism of Desire

Short-lived anemone, who made you?
   The sun made me.

Who wound the wind with orange blossom?
   The child in you the sea first talked to.

Who blanketed the hills with poppy gold?
   Just another maestro like you.

Where are your ancestors hidden?
   A blazon of stars, a smear of mist.

What is birth and what is death?
   Everything to dove fish kelp.

And you, traveling woman, how old are you?
   Like wine, it depends upon which country.

What is this world?
   Mercury tongue, music of snow
   only sometimes translatable.

Who was your mother?
   I never really knew her—hands of fire, smoky veil.

And your father, your brothers?
   They stand at the edge of water-sky,
   gray wind, whale spout.

Where does magic live?
> *In fields of wild hydrangea*
> *on a hill that opens into salty sky.*

Who will teach you to sing?
> *Sacred currents, inner rocking.*

How will you live?
> *Like swallows, like snow over stone.*

THE VOICES

The Calling

*"Never be so focused on what you're looking for
that you overlook the thing you actually find."* —Ann Patchett

In the beginning

she ran for the morning bus
in dark green jumper and saddle shoes.
She followed the rules: *two napkins with lunch,
sit with crossed ankles, stand with a graceful lift.*

After school she waited on the corner of Western
and Selby with old Mr. Ivory, the janitor from Ireland.

I cannot live in my own land, Miss, he told her.
Neither can I, she thought.

Believing

she was part of a long line of women.
Called to she didn't know what,
she bought a rickety wooden trunk at Goodwill,
painted it shiny black and loaded it
with what she was told to bring—white undershirts,
cotton underpants, black cotton knee highs,
comb, brush. She added her eyelash curler.

Sky in her head she made herself invisible
to see more clearly, to knock at kitchen windows
where day gathers in ordinary hymn,
looking for the sunlight, a sign of god.

Long months,

rows of beds,
each one cloaked with white curtains,
shadows of her sisters behind them.

Insomnia nested in her restless limbs.
At night she played Mozart in her mind,
walked the halls, prayed to painted Marys.

Tried to open invisible doors,
to read silence, her mother tongue,
the present absent.
Somewhere the world must be alive.

Long days trying to pray in chapel,
wanting and waiting to hear that voice,
the one she was sure had called her.
Watcher of dreams, a dream invented,
she opened eyes to the earth's marine and jade.

All harbor,

she steals chants from waves.
Even if she doesn't hear, she knows.
If that voice once called, it calls her always,
like moon and stars, light traces left inside her.

Paris: Meditation in Notre Dame Cathedral

Before us
          Behind us

You are the one who calls the women
to this dark church.

You, scarlet footsteps of setting sun
moving up dark columns
inside Notre Dame—that great womb.

You carry our sorrows—
the sorrow of women whose babies died,
women whose mothers died in childbirth,
whose men went to war,
whose men beat them,
women who couldn't read or write,
women who wrote in secret,
women who could not own,
who were owned.

Women who watched history written,
whose ideas men took and turned into law
or poetry, sojourners from far places
who never saw home again,
who nursed babies on bunks in the deep hold,
women who lost their own language,
forced to speak another's,
women who invented tongues and songs,
who sang the songs to children,
women who prayed, who cursed,
who were stoned.

We bless them as they pass through us.
We shout their dark sorrows.

Before me
> *Behind me*

You are the one I looked for as a child
first thinking you might be a nun
who taught me in school
where I breathed the notes
of their chant.
You in the budding apple orchard
behind the convent
outside me—and inside
flickering light at the edge of everything.

Lady in the cathedral
Voices in the dark
Teach me to listen.

Letter to Vincent

One may make a poem simply by arranging colors.
(Van Gogh in a letter to his sister)

1

In Provence we live on color
in white washed rooms, gold flecked air
enters us like pollen.

I trudge up steep hills
for bread and creamy cheese,
my tongue a stone

until I bite and my mouth fills
with new colors—citron, champagne.

2

The meadow a vast temple
open to the sky.

A Romanesque church
crowns each hill village,
cool in the heat,
wine in a cask, vermilion, tile red,
black cat sleeping on top.

Between heavy vineyards,
over white mountains.
Light on ochre walls
on red sand on violet rock,
June's eyes open.

3

Red-orange clay on soft yellow
stones, walls, cottages, barns.
In Roussillon every russet building
burns against solid azure.

Swallows swoop and trill against
ruby cherries in green nests.

4

We ask:
Who dreamed lavender fields?
Who first planted them?
Who saw early evening,
after a day of blues?

In the last of the mist
languidly rising from lavender,
Vincent speaks to us.

The Wall

Van Gogh, St. Paul's hospital, St. Remy

...working one's way through an invisible wall that seems to stand between what one feels and what one can do. (letter to Theo)

"YOU ARE NOT AN ARTIST, YOU ARE NOT..."

Laughter echoes from monastery walls,
from my pulsating mind.

I watch wheat stretch into the sky
through this prismed window.
   Stained glass like a partition
   between my heart and the world...

Through the asylum's walls,
through my wounded ear
I hear wildflowers rise and billow.
In the stone-walled field
roots unfurl, curl, stems limber,
sleek, free as that eccentric iris.

In my limbs the rocking
of lavender in wind
olive trees, cypresses
solid ochre of the Alpilles.

"YOU WILL NEVER BE AN ARTIST..."

At the easel, I am
a peasant bent over wheat,
under a bundle of grain.
My body, the bowed back of a miner.

I remember them slumped around the table,
ashy tubers dug from frozen ground,
roasted in coal slash, the blood-heat
melting snow around each hut.

"YOU WILL NEVER. . ."

My attendant, a stiff fellow
with his ring of keys and recitations —
what one can do and cannot do—
follows me out of doors
into the cloister garden, where I wrestle
the NOT and the NEVER,
into silence, where I weep
for moss trampled beneath my boots.

NEVER...

Wherever I go, newborn yellows
boil into earthly gold
touched with holy blue
like the sea at Saintes Maries
lit from inside.

Dragonflies harry white roses.
In the eye of my eye
the fiercest yellow on earth
ignites.

My hand stays in that flame
until I begin the sky.
Blue spatters all over my arms.

Outside, I can barely control my brush,
wild animal with its startling will
forms clouds, banks of poppies, tulips
shivering in sheer disbelief, under my fingertips.

I fall to my knees
as the sky convulses around me.
I laugh and inside, a bit of wall crumbles.

> *One must undermine the wall and grind
> through it slowly and patiently. (letter to Theo)*

A Poem for Two Voices: Seeing Her

Her face is her body

    The veil must cover

some enjoy looking

    my face, the space between my eyes

Once like an opal

    reveals the distance between

now asymmetrical

    my breasts

They look through me

    If they see my cheeks

invisible

    they will see how firm, how round

my body, this concavity

    I would be in their mouths.

edge or margin

    My mouth is

hollow vessel or cavity

my vagina, I must take care

the edge of a wound

not to laugh, not to widen

Two fleshy folds surround

this space, this darkness

the outermost layer

where they will know me

door for living words

agape, open

rind of kiwi, ripe pelt

I imagine abandon

Life!

Leaving, entering

Winter Orchards

Casa de Maria Retreat Center

1

Orange and yellow fruit hardens,
sycamores' bare ghosts
dance against a light shot sky.

Live oaks tremble in deep shine,
a shiver runs along the benches
looking for a spine to run up.

An ancient bristlecone pine
twists with sagging bark
more powerful than sculpture or word.

2

My book opens to the song
for the lady carved in granite
sister who comes in dreams.

Poetry enters darkness to find
a woman standing at the altar,
singing I AM to the alabaster saints.

I remember how paintings of women
fill the walls of the great hall at Avignon
in what was once the palace of the pope.

3

I remember nuns who taught me to be silent.
They named me Genevieve, the saint whose fire
saved Paris from the Huns.

I called myself Oxalis,
candle for December's full moon.

By Way of Words

Locked within the radiant metal skin
of a DC 10, in flight from one life
to another, I stare out a scratched
porthole to my Midwest,
twilight coming on.

Below, through miles of cloudless air,
a freeway cloverleaf glitters, a brooch.
Sweet planet of my youth,
my childhood. Where's home?

From the memory room of my brain,
Seamus Heaney's voice lilts:

You are neither here nor there,
A hurry through which known and strange things pass. . .

I am a vessel, of music,
assigned to Seat 11A, moving
mid to west above the continent
in the vacant space once called God's.

To the plane's blinking wing, I give
Yeat's *Stolen Child*—all of it,
Bishop's *Moose*—the start of it,
nimble music of Hopkin's *Wreck*—part of it:

Thou knowest the walls, altar and hour and night
The swoon of a heart that the sweep and the hurl of thee trod...

The flight attendant comes by for trash
and Eliot intones in my head:

Because these wings are no longer wings to fly
But merely vans to beat the air...

The captain's voice announces our descent.
I turn back to my fertile window.

Teach us to care and not to care...

First the desert of small LA house tracts,
then the light studded spines of buildings
slowly rise into view.

I think Emily here—her certain slant
waiting traffic stalled at salt rimmed lights,
tiny boats and rising lace-fringed sea swells.
With Neruda I want—

to be, and be nothing but light in the dark.

Scarlet sunset stripes the seaside hills,
the flag of a country made of smog and beauty.

Mother Tongue

for Bridget

All you know these early days is calling
mother, father, sister.
Sometimes a bird gurgle of bliss,
a scrap of music—
enough to make cups of ears.
Sounds chained in bracelets, glistening
objects, bright and dark—
gifts for your mouth, that temple of new sounds.
Your cries, your moving tongue's wild script.

Your wide eyes search in a green-scape,
for trees, bushes, hedges, boundaries blurred
between earth and sky, day and night.
Ahead of you, child, are names
of things and things not yet named.
Ahead of you, mallards and ducklings,
hawks and their chicks.
Inside, you live the names for every bird
and all the tender words we give you

so you can make your way
through the glittering world.

Line's End

A dot. A period. Lonely.
The mind rushes
to the text, the Capital

fearing that blank
between the clatter of one phrase
and the clang of the next.

Words, flashlights we swing
against caliginous dark.

Sounds fly over the earth
guiding us through silence.

Ahead, faces of the beloved dead,
round passage overflowing
with awe or grief

into a woods
        a stone circle
                a clearing.

Orange Light

of the California poppy
fallen among succulent leaves,
wings of the monarch in green wind,

from the dragging wing of a mourning dove,
from pelican hurling himself like a stone
out of the sky.

Flaming brilliance

from century leapers,
things that are fire
holding as much as possible—

Mozart's notes scratched
    on *Handel's Messiah*,
Monet's amber haystacks
    weighty as houses of parliament.

Luminescent flicker

singing over the ocean when no one
lies awake listening.
All the water drums fall silent—
then thunder!

Light of bright spirits

aureoles where heat gathers,
fervid heart of music;
all the poets who ever lived
all their voices at once!

Of Water

Baptist

For Conrad

I am busy on the riverbank
counting monarchs, watching baby turtles.
Suddenly your cry—a spear in my side!
I stroke your wounds, counting and naming
the dry seas, the craters and plains.

You are buckskin in patches, salty, speckled like a sky.
Afterward, I wash you in the muddy Mississippi,
release your sins to live with the carp
hiding in their church of reeds.
I slip a silk shirt over your thin, grieving shoulders.
Your eyes—wheel shafts of aquamarine.

I warn you, my heretic, the sun can be ruled by dark.
Knife-eyed heron stalks the day, spears its prey
scattering the tiny fish. Desperate with its own intent
yellow-eyed red tail kite twitches each nervous feather
in the precious seconds before a killing dive.

You are my blue   beloved   slipping
into narrow shadows that separate
dragonflies from cruel burning acacia.

River and Bear

*Look for the Bear and follow the Star,
my grandmother said—you'll always
find your way home.*

1

I started on West Seventh until a direction
took me. Where the river breaks into white
plunging without harness,
I walked to find the Bear.

But the orbit of earth whirled me
and stood me before the Cross.
I wanted the Lion and Hare in my arms.

2

The Dipper scoops liquid dark
into its bright cup, holds this vessel
to the mouth of the North to drink.

I carry my infant granddaughter to the window
hold her high above my head and say,
This is your cup.

3

Long ago when the buds of the lilac
were turning to ice,
I took her father's hand and walked out
past the Norway pines

to name the animals: the Bull, the Bear.
I showed him the twin stars in the handle
of the Big Dipper and how to find
his way home.

The Milky Way is a snow covered river
where North touches the handle
of the Little Dipper pouring
ice shards into the Big Dipper.

His eyes followed the white bird moon
to the nest of his Seven Sisters.

4

I turn to the old woman
asking for visions.
In her eyes I see my own face.
My hands that are empty.

Like deer in the woods
my spirit hands look for water.
This is my exile: to walk
country to country.
North to the river of light.
North to the cup of the Bear.

The Globe from the Deck
of the Hurtigruten Coastal Steamer

I stand on the deck of this ship.
Northernmost sea, islands float nearby
lit by midnight sun.
Out here, the North Sea is all there is.
Above Trondheim ice drifts
in the Arctic Ocean, with white whales
and white furred seals.

Then the Barents Sea, flotillas of grayling,
just behind the Arctic, armadas of solid ice
headed for the North Pole.
Past the North Pole
the gale force winds of the Beaufort.
I can see all the way to Alaska.

Below Alaska, I ride south
over the Pacific, like the albatross gliding,
over ice drifts in the Antarctic
to open water in the South Atlantic
where springs of blue cod well up.

Seawater stops along the belly of Africa
where, just above shimmering beaches
red fish gleam in the Mediterranean.
Turkey simmers at the Golden Horn
where the world collides.
The Black Sea thick
with schools of white sturgeon.
Just behind, Russia howls
dressed for perpetual snow.

Finland stretches, long, icy
as a bottle of Vodka. Above Finland,
the loaf of bread that is Norway.
Below the Norwegian sea,
the North Sea, planed and chrome-plated
beneath a silver dome of clouds.

I stand on the highest tier of this Coastal Steamer
riding the waves of the North Sea,
alone with myself at three in the morning
winding among gray stones and pale stars.

I Could Come to You as Water

Through familiar
pines and parting branches,
I come upon a brook,
dark and narrow slit
of water.

Watch your step
upon the stones,
green and slick
with moss and time.

Look deep into that chasm.
Let your cold hands remember
fire, remember the face
in falling snow.

Someplace further on,
water becomes a river
with shores you know.

Still further
        a sea
                lifts to the moon

where your hands remember
everything.

Song for the Rhone

Because you don't flow through my childhood,
I don't swim your currents.
On your banks archeologists find
Roman helmets, a goddess with a snake at her feet.
Because you are birdsong in the summer,
you are memory and your vowels chant
a prayer I cannot understand.

Because upstream tributaries
tell you of coming storms
or predict love in the meadows.
Because Avignon rose above you
full and fat and golden and I walked
the bridge, dreaming
late sunset fire castles in your depths.

Life dwindles slowly, without our knowing.
The force of your waters runs into the sea.
In you, creek water spills toward salt,
slowly carves pebble into sand grain,
cuts a delta through plateaus of sand.

Rhone, you leave behind villages of clay,
garnet vineyards, goshawks.
And ahead—gulls and the green
white expanse of Mediterranean,
where waves swallow river,
whisper *Rhone, Rhone. . .*
to longing rocks on the shore.

Winter Solstice: A Triptych

1

White acres of glint
cross a knife blade sea

all the way to the end of the year
as though there might not be another.

Slivers of light dance
off sharp waves

a low tide pointillism
stippling the western flank of rock.

The solstice draws its net
over the blue hillside.

2

I splinter in all directions
rushing to lose myself, drink in

crimson, alizarin west, ocean
lapis and plum, lavender islands—

colors go straight to my heart.
I want these slanting hours

to take their sweet time so I can
hold their incandescence

return to early things, scent of fir,
the wind steeped in indigo.

3

Inside me, old as mazarin starlight,
tongue I need in winter.

When my dreams lose their footage
I dig in my heels, feel gorse seeds settle.

Night unfolds on water,
between stone and flesh.

Distance so great it's not.

Welder

Starfall meeting of torch and hull,
white fireworks
explode from the freighter
against a winter carnival sky,
in the dark, ice sculptures.
I watch from a window
thinking of the welder at work in that wind.

Behind the boat, the bridge bucks and rises.
Trucks and cars roll over the arch
like a necklace of rosary beads,
a cold mathematics,
reminding me of my statistics teacher
who filled the board with formulas
as he talked non stop. I thought he spoke
a different language, like a poem in Irish.
When I listened, I heard patterns I could recognize.

Now as I go round the mysteries—fears and losses
sicknesses, good byes, letting go—
I am looking for patterns in ice, in fire,
spinning from planet to eye.

The welder will finish, the air will turn
bread colored, and the freighter will sail
from this harbor toward Sault Sainte Marie.

Until then we live in a blur
of blue and white—
more light, snowing.

Remembering Paris: Winter Light

I want to write of Paris, it's tarnished winter light,
but my eyes move to my own street, neither broad nor famous.

I want to write of anything but the honey locust in my yard.
We are friends, of course, know one another as tree and woman.

But narrow winding left bank streets,
flagstone that centuries run roughshod over—
this is what the blue hour calls for,
not these houses squatting across the frozen pond.

I want to hold awhile the grail of elsewhere—
small hotel desk manned by helpful Patrick,
wooden stairs to our dollhouse room,
small bath entered sideways.

The honey locust alive with invisible beads
is the soul of the winter where we die
yet above me the sky exposes the deepest blue
I could reach forever into,
my hand covered with leaves and birds.

What looks withered wears the invisible.
Not the moon of Paris over Seine but this shy thing
cloud veiled, homeless in a makeshift field of stars.

Rock From Skye

When I looked in the tide pool mirror on Skye,
it returned the smile of a young woman
who walked across the beach
from the empty one room school.

A rock's flecked weight caught my eye.
I picked up the shard, put it to my ear.
Basalt hunk sliced and thrashed long ago
from mountain to Irish sea and back to wild shore,
echoed with the voices I thought
were Celtic womens' wails—
No more, no more.
Chain of women forged by waves
frigid wind, vile gods, child-bearing bodies.
So I captured it and brought it home.

I hold its rough greyness,
rock chipped to the round shape
of Mother Goddess or Buddha,
thick thighs and arms I could climb,
sit in, hear the cosmos in its round head,
a gothic weight, my mute communion.

The Gift

In golden midsummer cotton grass
I hunch behind a wind-dwarfed pine
to watch a female moose and her calf
high step from forest to shore.

She lifts her head, long ears twitch
as she inhales inhabitants of a wind
that blows my way so I stay hidden
in my human smell.

Mother and calf bend to drink.
The water, rusty with iron, lies still,
between clumps of reeds.

Liquid rainbows yield to lapping tongues,
flow under velvet to become
marsh light in the eye of the moose.

I see the cotton grass let go.
Gathering, rising—the spirit of each waterhole
deserts its body to ghost over the marsh

like Christ on a church wall ascending.
I know salvation is not the blood of the lamb
but in the blood of a woman when her rivers flow.

In a room golden with morning and moose light
my children emerge from my dark waters.
I give them the river wide after thawing.

HOLY OILS

Holy Oil

Pigeons' breasts shine
like oil on wet streets

bodies built of balanced stones, sentries
line the tar flecked beach,

flints of gemstones,
reflections of rose windows,
creases in the bed sheet,

the oily coffee in my cup
turning white with real cream,
the label on our wine bottle,
attar of rose, essence of jasmine—
how full my glass,

finger prints on my mother's last card
her spidery "With love,"
black smudges of engine grease
lining my father's nails,
the shine of sacramental oil
on his forehead as he died,

slide of lavender oil
over wounds of body and soul,

wild horses in the French Carmargue,
white manes blowing in sea wind,
mothers nursing dark colts shining with sweat,
thousands of flamingos in the salt flats,

my brother wounded in the war,
he won't talk to me.

I would anoint the faces of those I love
with the oil that weeps
from my own skin.

Lascaux

Nineteen millennia ago

Behind the great hall of the bulls
hidden in a small recess
a woman used moss, colored ochre,
sticks of charcoal to make a herd
of spotted horses gallop across a cave wall.
Working in a flicker of light the artist
traced a curve with a shaved chalked twig,
filled in with a paste of charcoal
and two kinds of hard, dark earth.

She ground red ochre to a fine powder
with mortar and pestle, picked up a hollow bone,
then blew, mouth filled with bitter taste,
using her hand so thick lines of color
could meet without blurring, horses dappled
by stenciled dots and fingerprints dipped in paint.

Always in motion these ponies thunder
across the rock face, fresh as if just drawn.
I think I hear them snort and gnar,
feel their grassy breath,
or someone blowing pigment in the dark.
Was the painter surprised by what emerged?
Would she be amazed to know they are still here,
cantering in the dark, in the dawn?

Sunflower

Van Gogh 1888

Only a close up of a sunflower
turns to scales of trout or salmon,
ancient patinas or flints of gems,
smell of honey,
rough amber that rises
from strangling vines.

What were you longing for
when you made them?
Tawny flowers, summer wheat,
autumn grapes.

I am guided by color, you said, by light—
only they can undo or save me.

Bright yellow burns from inside out
as the sky turns turquoise.
This sunflower stabs me
with a living eye,
makes me see how everything
means something else.
Is something else.

Flowers of France

Poppies

Flowers of ruin,
flowers of stone,
poppies warm old walls.

Rising from a field of blood,
small flames tremble as we pass.

Their fiery petals stitch
embankments, loop through ditches
where we walk the edge of town.

By the wayside, in rainy furrows, under
waning sun, poppies.

Blackthorn

Nobody calls blackthorn *flower*
trailing for miles along rail lines,
and tag-ends of fields, until

suddenly black twigs burst
into white petals, outsized thorns.

Geraniums

The names of the men
carved into dark granite,
sculpted in the local
veined marble,
deep pink sandstone
over red geraniums.
Men who died for nothing
on the mud choked Somme
at Ypres, Verdun.

A hundred years later
they seem younger, not older,
the years between us shorter.

The long flower chain

made from daisies, violets, phlox
loops itself over barbed wire,
breaks, strews blossoms.
Seeds burn like teeth in the mouth of war.

Remembering Paris: Tapestries

When you remember me, speak of that French summer.
Talk of Andrew, Carlos and Bernardino
in the stone courtyard, speaking the language of boules.
I'm good at telling them what I mean,
my son says, his bright eyes dancing,
showing how he hits an imaginary ball.
They like to play war, like us, but they don't call it war.
All afternoon the thump of rubber on stone.
Outside the heavy courtyard door, traffic roars.
Paris for Andrew is two Spanish boys who throw
balls between the iron railings of his balcony —
balls which he must return.

· · ·

When you talk of me, remember Timothy at Cluny,
his mind suddenly able to roam across centuries.
He stops in front of every portrait asking
Was he good or was he bad?
We pore over illuminated manuscripts,
where icons gleam—a world passing into a world to come,
emblems in lapis, in carnelian.
He traces over a crown of gold clasped by two snakes,
a curving arm filled with demons and winged lions.

In a book of hours, we study symbols of the Zodiac.
In my birth month, April,
a peasant carries a green branch to water.
I know I will carry a green branch for Timothy,
a memory—sitting on marble steps
in a hall hung with unicorn tapestries,
naming flowers, fruit, herbs, kings, queens, wars—
names and eras rising from the salty pages of our tongues.

• • •

At the Invalides a military funeral for French soldiers,
black garbed women cry across the courtyard.
My sons spend all afternoon studying ancient weapons,
the jeweled carvings on swords and battle axes.

They're works of art, Timothy proclaims.
Nowadays, weapons aren't works of art, are they?

At the Grand Palais, crowds worship a painting by Manet.
A young man turns his back on his parents,
rejects the breakfast that his mother made.
On a chair beside him, an ancient sword and helmet,
but the enormous eyes in his marble face
look far beyond the room, past gazing art lovers,
fixed on the clarity of his own death.

I know I'll come back to Paris some day,
if war doesn't come too soon.

Of Trains and My Father

Trains and my father
moved together
breathed together
a steady rhythmic motion
his schedule certain
a train's coming and going
morning departure
with clinking lunch pail
evening arrival
heavy with train grease.

In long underwear
thick gloves
my father walked
the boxcar canyons
his breath in engine steam
his energy
oil poured into steel.
At home he was quiet
each day
a little more shell-like.

Wind lover
wheel lover
bluffs over tracks
junkyards
train towns
broken parts
wrench
nut
bolt lover
your fingers
tasted engines
mechanic.

Does your spirit walk
deserted train yards searching
for the years left there?
At home you were so quiet
the empty quiet of a train
after a long journey.

Dining Room Table: Ways of Seeing

My dining room table, a crack in the center,
winding paths through the wood
carries me north and south,
backward and forward in time.

· · ·

We are visiting Zoyla in the Guatemala mountains.
She shows us her new table,
dark finished wood with ladder back chairs,
polished and strangely suburban,
with legs that grip a dirt floor
in the same room as the cooking-fire
under a window cut into a wall of concrete.

Did her husband leave before
they could finish the floor?
Now she's turned
the front room into a little store,
selling bright weavings, peppers and beans
to feed and dress her children.

· · ·

When I was a girl, I heard chaos
but not the small comforting sounds.
My brothers kicked and punched through every meal,
father silent, mother angry, all of this beneath
a portrait of Jesus in agony, a dark garden.
His bloody sweat, his suffering, seasoned our food.

• • •

Just married, we bought the antique oak table
from an old widower.
We loved our table's heavy clawed feet,
the talons of a mythical bird.

• • •

When Andy sat at our big oak table
with his homework, I stood over him
making him write each word. *One more
sentence*, I'd say. *And one more.*

• • •

After my mother died, I'd cook
Thanksgiving dinner for Dad and my brothers
who sat at the table while I worked.
At my father's place,
the cloth's still stained with cranberry.
I remember how he loved to eat
and died refusing food.
He left so little—I don't want to scrub the spot away.

• • •

In the mountains of Guatemala
Zoyla, Mayan weaver, smiles at me
with more joy in her shining table
than I ever knew in mine.

Lamp, Boat, Ladder: A Samhain Triptych

After Rumi

1

Nothing in mid-country dust
     but leaf drift.
Scoured cottonwoods inscribe calligraphies
     on parchment air.
In rabbit, squirrel, fox hush
     only half heard thrashings.

Wind shifts what's visible,
     trembles pond
where cattail quills shiver.

The nutshell of infinite space
     unbuckles.
Goose moon waits
     behind laced branches, Celtic coils,
the face of an owl.

2

From the Irish west, a spirit burns
a boat flames on the sea,
reflection truer than real

the way once, not the condor,
but her shadow crossed
the face of a juniper.

3

Gone
leaf from the maple
      heron from the rookery
            cicada from wild mustard.

Those who are not here
drift here.

Tin roofs, oil lamps in the windows,
as the boat burns
even the stones, the water.

Reverse Migration

Written with Roseann Lloyd

November in Minnesota.
The descent has deepened
from dark to dark
beneath trees that tell us nothing.
Work the only way out.

I stay inside as much as possible.
I write. Weavings I brought from
Guatemala help another season
migrate.

In El Colibri, the hummingbird
shop of women weavers
with pulse quick fingers,
with patience to take two months
to weave a table runner.
The Violet Saber Wing
of the Mayan past
mates with the Purple Throated
jewel colors of hummingbirds
of the rainforest.

The descent has deepened
from dark to dark beneath
trees that tell us nothing until April,
color being the only way out.
Humming colors,
sun struck fuchsia and orange
trumpet vine shrimp flowers,
hibiscus, papaya, lavender jade,
Green Crowned Brilliant.

Some say hummingbirds
are the moon in disguise
trying to seduce the sun.

Some say the Spanish imposed these designs
to separate the Mayan people into villages.
Women resisted, created new colors
that made the design their own.

Some say hummingbirds
travel all over the world
on the backs of geese.

Steel wings carried weavings to Minnesota
where in November the descent has deepened
beneath trees that tell us nothing.
The only way out is patience,
the womens' pulse quick fingers,
colors that bring hummingbirds
North in November.

Doves

Drenched and disheveled
doves in the rain
descend with a dizzying drop.

Start with down feathers, moody skies
gray, white, blue, brown
strata of colors, water and air
heart and delicate lungs.

Continue with absence and thirst
for rain to spill down
for doves to alight
softly on this rock strewn beach.

You city-worn doves,
your last clutch of feathers
hopeless cloud cover.

Voices like small bubbling fountains,
wine-red feet, round little eyes,
endless savor and desire.

Doves in a fortress, doves
in cathedrals destroyed by war.
Scratching the gothic arches of Chartre.
Shuddering the bell tower at Albi.

Doves eluding peregrine falcons
flicker in evergreens and medieval ruins,
join the call to prayer in Istanbul.

An everywhere cry,
double chambered heartbeat
asking what we cannot answer—

Who who are you?
Inside, outside, echoes
in basalt, in limestone,
among stars.

The Song of Clay

Ankara Turkey

In the Archaeological Museum,
a clay tablet carved in Sumerian
for Ningirsu, god of fertility.

Soft etches, lift of riverbed
where the waters shine.
Cedar branches brush blue sky.
Dusky wings of bats careen
from branch to branch.
Wind sighs the sound of clay
shaped to carry a human voice.

Maybe it says

> *The phosphorescent float of sky*
> *we hold between us*
> *touches the undersides of trees.*

Maybe it says

> *We become a riverbank*
> *where night animals bend*
> *to ease their thirst.*

Tonight will bring luminous dreams.
Above this terra cotta,
above us as we sleep,
holy oil lights every tree.

Emblems of Earth

Season of the Swan

The doe hesitates behind trees,
steps into snow filled meadow.
I could take a bucket, fill it
with the tracks of her small hooves.

Touching an oak, I become an oak.
Watching a deer, I become a deer
walking across to the saltlick.
If I watch deer drink,
I am the tang on their tongues.

Once I drank from a clean
northern river, tasting granite,
moss, moose, a trace of rabbit,
grouse, the prints of weasel and quail.
As sun broke over rock
mountains melted and rivered
in my mouth.

You waded up the river,
knew the piney silence
of green forests,
skipped a stone, watched the circles
lave and loop and spend.

Now we wash our hands,
break the bread
and lift our cups
to the canopy of leaves.

I want to call you,
lick water from your hands
but I can't say your name.
Reach with me into night.
This space—
I could give you this space.

On the narrow bed I think of our first night.
Beneath your hands, I became a brook,
your tongue on pebbles.
Now we are swans.
We close our eyes and dive.

Love in the North

We are all just walking each other home. —Ram Dass

So new for me to hear cicadas
loud as the sea at high tide.
Magical things always happen
when light travels north.
Birches engorge like a room in a dream,
the same room you wake up to.

Now flocks of rootless people,
salmon, and moose are vanishing.
Tomatoes, olives, the women
who harvest them,
vanishing—
on the ground beneath snow
ashes of berries and leaves.

Sometimes, when the snow melts,
everything hidden comes clear
and the soul can be seen—maybe
like this wooden box, splintered
and gouged, the one I've carried
for such a long wandering.

Sometimes, with your hand tucked
into mine like a baby bird,
we stop in a kale patch no one has tended,
follow the sound of a dried up stream,
peel off some birch bark and eat it.

The box becomes the room
filled with coral, turquoise, jade,
my grandmother's ruby ring,
an icon from Mary's house,
a little lapis glass bottle.
Open, and a scent fills everything
like the midnight sun
making sleep and death
impossible to remember.

Lilacs: Triptych from the Cold

1. Minnesota

May begins as lilacs ladle purple into green.
I grow young, swim in their deep scent,
their liquid sound, swim past all my springs,
return to the old city, my old joys—
boys driving by in eternal parade,
motorcycles, Chevies, Fords,
girls throwing flowers on what roars.

2. Vermont

Weeks of bleak scrawn,
then May's scent of arrival.
Petals jumble a room filled with light.
A man and woman
naked and facing each other.

Three shades of purple in these lilacs
long brushes of evening,
mountain calyces
fragile as agate,
the last closest to the smell of white—
frost a star edges with its fire.

3. Norway

The fiord as shiny as metal.
Regardless of June weather,
it always reflects a cloud cover
so you never feel up to carving
your heart in its water.

Where no citrus trees bloom,
where swallows never fly,
summer is almost somber with sun.

A man reads on the train platform.
Lilacs brush his head and arms.
Oh Lavender One, hovered by lilacs
while I stand watching
the train, the white night.

Border Crossings

Elder blossoms spill at the border crossing.
Saxifrage splits the pavement.
Dandelions' tasseled crowns reign
over unused lanes of empty customs kiosks
where roadblocks slow you down
and no one waves you through.

Willkommen in Deutschland.
Bienvenue en France.

France polices its borders
with Italy to keep out immigrants.
But the clouds wander from San Marino
to Bergamo, to Padua and Ravenna.
Erasing all borders
the Rhine, heaves its way north
sluggish between factories
below castle walls.

Joyous, the Rhone
rushes to the Mediterranean
from Swiss alps,
drunk on its own youth.
Through vineyards river pours hues of wine—
peony, garnet, amber, cherry
red as a stained glass window
swirling Chagall vision, jeweled partition
between then and now.

We crossed many European borders—
German guards scared us
Italians waved us on.

*1980 in the Alps between Italy and France
our children collected thousands of lira
from the money changer.*

*1970 crossing the border on our way to Munich
hitch-hikers hid in our car.
We held our breath, heard the drum of our heartbeats
as the guards slowly studied our passports.*

Now, golden flowers hold their ground
against wars to come, rivers of blood.
Elder, saxifrage, dandelion
the milk of their stems, drop by drop
replenishes the ancient
worn-out land.

Remembering Paris: City of Light

"It's a cold and it's a broken hallelujah." —Leonard Cohen

In the station at suburban Bois de Colombes,
a young man from Zaire trudges toward us,
tall and muscular, yet needing our help
to lift heavy plastic bags to the platform
where his wife waits, cradling
a flowered enamel soup pot.

Our train speeds away from Colombes,
while he speaks to us about his life.
Trouble with my government, he says,
with the careful ambiguity of exile.
University students, just married,
forced to flee in the middle of the night.

*Now we have to move again. Trouble
with our apartment. I have searched for work
five months. There is nothing here for me.
My wife is pregnant.* Exhausted, she sits back,
staring at some invisible point in the air,
a mound of bags piled around her
holding everything they own. *Paris will be
our home now*, her eyes down, voice soft,
granite underneath every word.

As we arrive in Paris Gare Saint-Lazare,
five clocks strike at once.
The couple drag their bags between trains
into a smoke filled Bastille night
where taxis crawl among gyrating bodies.
Above them, a rain of fiery sparks.

Revelers force them to dance among exploding fireworks,
spray them with pink and green streamers.
We watch them disappear into waves of noise and color.
Behind closed doors, jazz plays softly, candles burn,
little tongues of flame cast into mirrors.
Too late to turn back.

The Open Window

Nice, France

Through shutters, an open air market
where a juggler tosses oranges,
fist sized peaches into shoppers' hungry bags,
loving the torrent of his own talk.
Women in line vie for his attention, roll their eyes
when an old one pushes to the front.

Slabs of salmon bake on terra cotta bricks,
peach and melon, slashes of mustard and olive.
Fish sleep in ice beds, eyes pasted black spots.
In black pots peppers sizzle and burn.
Everyone carries a brown loaf,
each pockmarked crust, the caul of a miniature monk,
as the horizon runs with raspberry juice.

The walls of our room are cool and white.
Lunch pulls us to the table—
burnt tapenade and a pastry puff,
with pureed cod and fraise,
grilled shrimp, aubergine with red sauce.
The outside world clatters
beneath an edible, steaming sun.
Rhubarb compote, vanilla glace for dessert.

White sheets warm the bed.
From the window light streams
through our bodies.

Vegetable Soul

Your soul is a chosen landscape. —Paul Verlaine

Or maybe the soul is a still life
like Cezanne's onions—crinkled skin,
astringent flesh, pungent breath
cushioned on a table like eggs in a nest.

They add depth to a stew
without becoming the thing
like the blue wash
that's part undercoat,
part shadow.

Onions dance, foliate fingers,
grab and clabber language,
green flames in the throat
of the wine bottle,
the molecules that make up my skin,
the air between our lips.

Or maybe the soul is edible, the inside
of a butternut squash that I split
with a crack of the blade,
scoop seeds, oil for the oven.
My hands, my grandmother's hands.
My mouth, my mother's mouth,
the singe on the tongue, the golden swallow.

A Break in the Hedge

1

If I slip my finger into foxglove,
into the lavender of heather,
I will hear the earth's deep hum.

2

Blue cornucopias of wisteria
pour over the balconies.
Bougainvillea guards the stairways.

3

A surge of poppies trembles
rising wind and purple lupine.

4

Hedgerow tucks a drop of fuchsia
into a twiggy pocket.

5

Rosettes, umbels, sepals play old love songs.
Their scattered notes fly over the earth.

6

This clouding over.
This hazing of the thistle.

7

Just before dark
three hollyhock stalks
nine violet stars.

8

Tall fennel's curly fronds
teach me to bow.

Chartres Cathedral

When you step inside stone
blinded by afterimage,
half-light leans through texts of glass
jewel stillness suspended.

Height, the fossil of a faith
that made these vaults ascend
like Dürer's hands,
touching at the apex.

No crucifixion scenes in this bare space,
cathedral soaring like a symphony.

If you struck one of the columns
with a tuning fork,
the whole edifice would sing
to the blue lady of stained glass.

Deep below the floor's labyrinth.
the holy well of the Celts,
once ruled by the subterranean virgin,
the basalt lady of the pillar.

Mother goddess Isis,
dark phase of the moon,
the soul forever cast in her image.

Ways of Singing

Joshua Bell Plays Mendelssohn

I wake to a stone circle
where he sways, music in his arms.
Light from a slivered moon
traces him against the black sea.

Deep in earth, undertones
rise from pounding roots.
Vibrato surges through his swaying.
Knees bend and straighten
with the surge, insurge
through his arms, fingers to the violin,
the stage, a cliff,
a tree in the wind of it.

His bow is a dowsing branch,
and I am dying of thirst.

Melody lifts my hair,
rises and rises over the bare hills,
tears at my heart, leaps up the moor,
cleaves a spring from stone.

One moonlit island night
I watched Prometheus, fire bringer,
arms chained to the rock behind him,
rage to the universe in archaic Greek,
his voice, tree bark, scrabbled and scarred.
I understood every word
the way I understand this music.

Wind and breath hold still,
no trembling leaf, no quaver.
In the quiet, a memory echo
of bells buried beneath the sea.

Praise

I want to praise what cannot last—
scarlet and orange leaves
crushed and trampled, the way
they rise again in wood smoke.

I want to think the way wind thinks
the way an oak leaf dreams
shadow and light, the way
blackbird builds her nest or a cloud
blooms out of emptiness.

I want to name things
the way the dwarf pine names
shining grubs beneath bark skin
the way nettles spark fever
the tawny owl calls feathers
under the new moon
secretly feeding earth and sun.

I tell my hand write like lichen
over stone, a bit of dry rot, a raindrop,
tell my eye imagine like a mirror,
my tongue to speak the mystery of salt.

I'm hungry for light
spread like gold-brown apple jam
on my skin.

Speak, but let things be
exactly as they are. How easily
they shelter alone, behind a stone,
how they steal into my ear
and whisper *death, go away.*

The Pleiades turn and return
as night hides us in her black velvet,
little lights, lives setting, rising on earth

AMONG STARS

Wild Tongues

I've watched for the Holy Spirit all day,
knowing she's there—could be the red finch
on my balcony, the badgering crow,
the gull dragging a curtain of sea mist.
She bending the grass, she the wind
tasting of orange flower and orange rind.

In the colors of poetry, wisdom hovers
in the held breath of my waiting.

Once I searched for her in libraries.
She, I could pray to, latch onto
like a duckling pipping
in her mother's wake.
Even as a child, I longed
to spend my life in praise.

Sometimes, I consider going back
to kneeling and bowing,
digging my nails into the back of a pew.
Instead I eat yogurt and drive to class
to help my students hear
whisperings, poems already
spiraling inside them.

The child I was looks back at me
from tired student eyes.
I want to feed the driving flames
that crater their minds and souls,
so I open all the windows.
We quake in spirit wind.

Insomnia

> *Weary, past midnight, who are you searching for?*
> "Questions for the Moon" by Ho Xuan Huong

You walk silent rooms after midnight,
wakefulness a signal turning inside you,
one of your inheritances, a keepsake
that holds the feathers, bones,
the moon of every night in your future.

You answer each of your questions with a question.
Its shadow falls into every corner of the house
followed by the spirits of everyone you've ever known.

You drift from window to window
barely touching the floor,
warming your hands with tea,
chamomile & ginkgo.

You listen to rose petals falling,
think *constellations, comets, lights of distant cities*
while watching your husband turn in his sleep.

Your love's sleep is a mirror
held up to another world
where everything disappears, wing and word,
as blue stars fall. But they don't brush you.

Some nights the grief of your body
makes love to its joys.
The moth drinks from the honeysuckle,
the moon nests in the aerie it makes from clouds.

You give up on sleep and cling to the hopes
of the wakeful, who count the bones of the sleeping
while they listen to the surf erase the shore,
making the dark their mirror.

The Blue Hour

Watery dreams roll through me,
someone's playing Mahler.

No, it's blackbirds swarming south,
abandoning their songbook trees,
individual notes gone mad.

Capes of shadow,
sparrows are footfalls.
Their song follows.

Thumb sized snowy plovers whir
a rushing cloud over the tide bed.

Their long bills clacking, dark eyed
egret sculptures shift
from one foot to the other.

Mockingbird mimics and repeats
his half improvised repertoire,
leaving green traceries, sleek spillways.

Slant of light—Persian and purple
turns rocks into reclining bodies.

The sea delivers restless speeches
"Run run run it's all ahead..."
then quickly changes direction.

At the end of Mahler's Fourth
the bows of the cellists are dousing rods,
the oboe's one note elides into silence.

Sleeping or waking
I see myself where I never thought to be.

Shell

A response to "Out There,"
a painting by Hérve Constant

A passion, older than we are survives
in blue herons, beach roses, sun trail
dusky coral in the late sky.

The part of us that has no alternative
to loss, dying desire, the body's changes.
The soul's roar and neigh, the spirit's
memory of words it wants to sing.

What reawakens love in us
could be anything—the way tulips mate
the colors of bees on anther, stamen,
wind rearranging the grace of pelican wings,
a child's voice on the telephone.

An animal amulet,
a secret hardened begging bowl,
something to curl the body into
when clouds rumble along the house
and bird-calls nail the ceiling.

Or a coquille shell pinpricked with light
that once floated among stars.

Night Songs

Windows across the courtyard go dark
in a silence marked by the call of a lone gull,
the turn and curl of moonless waves,
train shaking the building, the long whistle.

Night inverts like a mother
playing here and gone, drawing
a tight shirt over her child's eyes.

Night, pull your black shirt around this day,
over the beach walker, beach sleeper,
train watcher, crying baby.

Cover the refugee,
the migrant, the one who is beaten.
Gentle the dog-tired fathers, bone-weary mothers,
those who sleep back-to-back.

Sleep my granddaughters, you dreaming gymnasts.
Sleep wide eyed baby in your white crib.
Sirius paces the heavens.

Sirius plays Bach for those who cannot sleep.
Dark barges slide to nowhere over a stygian sea.
Cimmerian horses gallop toward a murky beach.

Turn away from analogue and digital;
turn away from time.
Face the beckoning night.
Sleep as the dark stars burn inside you.

In the Same Sky

When that illuminator Supermoon
pours silver over phosphorescent surf,

when darkness turns to flare path
or crests waves inside us,

when you lie with all your length
and warmth and weight over me,

the world is big enough
to contain us, small enough

that now and then, for the space
of a night, like Orion we can walk

the length and breadth of hemisphere
and be home again in time

to cook breakfast in the morning.

Remembering Paris: City of Visions

We enter monuments to the past,
Notre Dame, the Louvre, Sainte Chapelle.
If we pressed our ears to the ground,
we would hear silence gathering like time
as borders unstitch themselves,
as empires crumble into bits of grey stone.

While we pace the circuit of lights,
wars graze the edge of our consciousness,
ricochet back to their own countries.
In the brasserie, wine glasses break.

We listen for the roar
of tanks, but it's wind we hear,
a sullen advancing
while the earth cracks and peels
like a canvas of dreams.

City of losses, city of visions
larger than all our fears.
There's a storm on the way and we,
holding the hands of strangers
feel too small to push
a gale force back to sea.
How sorry we are to be only ourselves.

We slip inside cemetery walls,
search for a place where stone
whispers *peace   peace   peace.*

Out of My Hands

I walk out of the warmth.
Full moon and its corona,
great spill milky way
pouring from the tipped bowl of night.

I cup my hands as if to catch
cold water from a brook.
Let them fill with night,
hold the dark I try to drink.

When I lie down, arms outstretched
my body whirls outward.
Then wrinkled forehead, heavy breasts
belly, thighs round to a bowl.

I spin the way the universe spins
out of the cracked cups of my hands.

On Water, In Air

Because a voyager travels between stars.
Up there, to know what is between is to know.

Because the eagle turns upon the thermal, fiercely
elegant, even its smallest feathers hook air.

Because the sea hurries, foot on the treadle fast
your hand cannot hold what it contains.

Because flesh is lonely you listen to rock crabs burrow in sand.
Along the underbellies of rocks the sound of lines being carved.

Because magnetic clouds of plovers squeeze and spread out
like a giant thought, a watery burble of notes.

Because the moon is buried beneath eons of yearning
and rains our own longing upon us.

Because the wave repeats obsessed, the sharp attempts
of language wears away stone.

Where your hand was no longer is.
What is the sound for what's gone?

The Sound of the Bed

In flight over the Atlantic I saw sound
travel across a screen—green waves, green mountains.

The next morning we woke in a German farmhouse.
down comforter, feather pillows, your arms around me.
Flowers called pink fairies peeled off the walls.
The bed was next to a large window. All night
Orion held our sleep. We woke to light snow falling,
lay close without moving because the bed creaked.

Our shadows on the ceiling made a cross riding
down a ray of light through waves of mountains.
Beyond each arm stood dark pines.
Under the trees snow held a thousand cups,
in each cup a shadow and in each shadow—silence.
The bed, a rill, a running.
Only our breathing.

Pacific in Winter

These waves did I dream them?
Waves muddy with rain,
trailing wedding veils.
Didn't they write their rhythms
into my poems for years?
Didn't rocks undulate
to melodies of waves
planting their symmetries inside me?
Making me want to weep.
Making me jubililant.

Wherever I go, as long as I walk
hard paths, I want to breathe salt air.
Seventy years is a good age to turn and bow
to islands in the West,
snow-drifted mountains in the North,
East to the old pier, and South
to misty grey infinity.

Seventy years have taught me
patience, perhaps—how to watch
light through all its changes,
wanting what everyone wants—time
sharp and still as the air today
as I walk this narrow strip
between rocks and sea,
sand oozing under my footsteps,
my sleeves fluttering like wings
as though I could soar.
I can't fly but I'll keep on walking
with persistent strides
that have brought me this far.

About the Author

Mary Kay Rummel was the first Poet Laureate of Ventura County, CA. *Cypher Garden* is her eighth published poetry book, her sixth full collection. *The Lifeline Trembles*, was co-winner of the 2014 Blue Light Press Award. *This Body She's Entered*, her first book, won the Minnesota Voices Award for poetry and was published by New Rivers Press in 1989. Her work has appeared in numerous regional and national literary journals and anthologies and has received several awards, including six Pushcart nominations. Mary Kay has read in many venues in the US, England and Ireland and has been a featured reader at poetry festivals including Ojai and San Luis Obisbo, CA. She loves to perform poetry with musicians. A professor emerita from the University of Minnesota, Duluth, she and her husband, Conrad, teach part time at California State University, Channel Islands. They live and play with their grandchildren in California and Minnesota. marykayrummel.com

About the Cover Artist

Colleen McCallion is an artist from Laguna Beach, California. This is her fourth collaboration with Mary Kay Rummel after meeting at the Vermont Studio Center.

The cover oil painting titled "Resting Mother" represents the artist, the mother, tired from her duties, holding her "seedlings", her four children. The looming calla is her joy and her spirit, ever-present, even in sleep.

Notes

Thank you to California poet, Maia whose work has nourished mine for many years.

I acknowledge this debt of creative inspiration. The following poems in particular are indebted to her work:
Baptist—owes a debt to Blue Torpedo, italicized lines from *Blue Torpedo*.
The Wall owes a debt to *Fire*—italicized lines at the end of part 1.
Mother Tongue—owes a debt to her poem of the same name.
On Water, In Air—inspired by Answers Without Questions.
Vegetable—inspired by *Butternut*.
Symphony in Blue and Yellow—owes a debt to *Life to Death* and *Forgiveness*, Italicized lines in part 3.

Night Songs owes a debt to *Night* by Laure-Anne Bosselaar.

Holy Oil was inspired by Gail Peck's poem, *Prayer*.

A Break in the Hedge was inspired by Janice Moore Fuller's poem, *Through a Falcarragh Cottage Window*.

The quotes in *By Way of Words* are from the following poems:
Postscript by Seamus Heaney;
The Wreck of the Deutschland by Gerard Manley Hopkins;
Ash Wednesday by TS Eliot;
There's a certain slant of light by Emily Dickinson;
Carnal Apple, Woman Filled, Burning Woman by Pablo Neruda.

The cave at Lascaux is the famous site of prehistoric paintings in Southwestern France which are estimated to be from 15 to 17 thousand years B.C.

Hervè Constant, whose painting inspired Shell, is a London based French artist. www.hervèconstant.co.uk

Rocamadour, in Southwestern France, is a medieval pilgrimage site which houses an ancient Black Madonna.

Other Poetry Books by Mary Kay Rummel

The Lifeline Trembles, Blue Light Press, 2014, co-winner of Blue Light Press Award;
What's Left Is The Singing, Blue Light Press, 2010;
Love in the End: A chapbook, Bright Hill Press, 2008;
The Illuminations, Cherry Grove, 2006;
Green Journey, Red Bird, Loonfeather Press, 2000;
The Long Journey Into North: A chapbook, Juniper Press 1999;
This Body She's Entered, A Minnesota Voices Award Winner at New Rivers Press, 1989. Finalist for a Minnesota Book Award.

Storying: A Path to the Future, written with Elizabeth Quintero Peter Lang International, 2015

Recent Anthologies Containing Her Work Include:

St. Paul Almanac (Arcata Press); *Nimrod* (University of Tulsa); *Askew; Miramar; River of Earth and Sky: Poems for the 21st Century* (Blue Light Press); *Silk & Spice* (Pirene's Fountain, Glass Lyre Press); *Amore: A Collection of Love Poems*, (Johnny Tucker, ed); *Amethyst and Agate: Poems of Lake Superior*, (Holy Cow! Press.) *Creativity & Constraint*, (Wising Up Press); *Carrying the Branch: Poets in Search of Peace*, (Glass Lyre Press).

CPSIA information can be obtained
at www.ICGtesting.com
Printed in the USA
FSOW01n1059280617
35725FS